Love Mandalas

Mandala means circle in Sanskrit. This word is also known as wheel and whole. From the spiritual point of view, it is an energy center for balance and purification that helps transform the environment and the mind. It is like starting a journey towards your essence, it opens doors until now unknown and makes your inner wisdom sprout. Integrating them into your life will give you center and a sense of calm in the midst of storms. These mandalas are painted in watercolor; crayons and acrylics, and bring a special light to all who value it.

It is widely proven that painting is one of the best therapies that exist to calm the soul and mind. To paint mandalas it is always better to use colored pencils instead of markers, tempera or crayons, because the movement you make with these pencils produces a sound that induces relaxation. In addition, it is much easier to give different shades to the drawing even if you use a single pencil.

In addition to painting love mandalas, he proposes to make powerful affirmations for 21 days, which are the days when brain cells are renewed and new connections can be established, if you find it difficult to meditate in the traditional way, this may be a way to do it.

Thus, 63 love mandalas are delivered with their respective powerful affirmation, the first 21 mandalas are to promote self-love, increase your self-esteem, set affirmations that give you security in various aspects of your life. The 21 second mandalas are affirmations of a couple, either to attract a healthy love or to strengthen the one you already have, when you have them painted you can even give it away!. They are affirmations of healthy love, no the romantic love that hurts so much.

The last 21 affirmations are to cultivate compassionate love in yourself, the universal love for all that exists. You can imagine your heart at the center of your life, then those closest to you, and then turning to neighbors, coworkers, acquaintances, and finally strangers. This is your mandala of compassionate love.

Welcome to this loving mandalaventure.

MANDALAS AND AFFIRMATIONS FOR SELF LOVE

Affirmation day 1: I love and accept myself unconditionally.

9.

Affirmation day 2: I approve of myself and I feel great

Affirmation day 3:
I am a unique and special person

Affirmation day 4:
I accept praise from others easily

15.

Affirmation day 5:
I deserve all the good that life offers me

Affirmation day 6:
I release my need for suffering

Affirmation day 7: I feel very good about myself

Affirmation day 8:
I release my need to please others

Affirmation day 9:
I release my past and live in the present enjoying my life to the fullest

25.

Affirmation day 10: I am valuable and important.

Affirmation day 11: I feel love towards myself because I am unique

Affirmation day 12: I feel love towards myself because I am unique

Affirmation day 13:
I listen to the needs of my body

Affirmation day 14: I honor and respect my body

Affirmation day 15: I deserve health, vitality and peace of mind

Affirmation day 16: I believe that I can heal myself

Affirmation day 17: I am the creator of my life and my financial success

Affirmation day 18:
I am more powerful than any obstacle or circumstance

Affirmation day 19:
I have immense courage and I take action even in the face of adversity and fear

45.

Affirmation day 20: I am always willing to step out of my comfort zone to achieve the success that I deserve

Affirmation day 21: I am an expression of God and therefore I am love.

Note: If you are a non-theist, you can replace “God” with “Universe”.

MANDALAS AND AFFIRMATIONS OF COUPLE LOVE

Affirmation day 1:
If I love myself healthy, I can give healthy love.

Affirmation day 2: I radiate love and respect and I receive love and respect.

Affirmation day 3:
I attract / have people and situations that support and nurture me

Affirmation day 4: I trust my partner, just as he/she trusts me

Affirmation day 5: We rely on our projects

Affirmation day 6:
I admire my partner for his/her intelligence, kindness and generosity

I LOVE
YOU

Affirmation day 7: With my partner we can dialogue and reconcile differences without aggression

Affirmation day 8: My partner and I have common projects and we managed to achieve them

LOVE

Affirmation day 9: My partner and I respect our individual spaces

Affirmation day 10: With my partner we build a peaceful and harmonious relationship

71.

Affirmation day 11: love is not a feeling it is a daily practice

Affirmation day 12:
“Love is not looking at each other but rather looking both in the same direction”.

The Little Prince

Affirmation day 13: "You will know that they really love you when you can show yourself as you are without fear of being hurt"
Walter Riso

77.

Affirmation day 14:
"The person I love is an important part of my life, but not the only one".
Walter Riso

Affirmation day 15:
I love you and I don't need you, but I choose you

Affirmation day 16: Find a partner when you're ready, not because you feel lonely

83.

Affirmation day 17:
To love is not to lose individuality, it is to reaffirm yourself next to the other.

Affirmation day 18:
To love is to grow in pairs, being different and unique.

LOVE
you

Affirmation day 19: We accept ourselves, we do not "approve" ourselves, loving is not judging.

Affirmation day 20:
"The important thing is not how much they love you, but how they do it".
Walter Riso

Affirmation day 21: We all deserve a beautiful love, a love that is in good times and bad, understanding, that does not judge, real.

Note: note: write your name and that of your partner, or you and me in the box.

MANDALAS AFFIRMATIONS OF COMPASSIONATE LOVE

Affirmation day 1: “Compassion towards others begins with kidness toward oneself”.

Pema Chödrön

Love

Affirmation day 2: Compassion begins with service to the others.

Affirmation day 3:
“I am compassionate, because every person I come across is fighting a tough battle“
Platon

Affirmation day 4: “If I want others to be happy, I practice compassion. If I want to be happy, I practice compassion”.

Dalai Lama

Affirmation day 5:
“Compassion becomes real when we acknowledge our shared humanity”.
Pema Chödrön

Affirmation day 6:
"Spirituality is recognizing and celebrating that we are all inextricably connected".
Brené Brown

107.

Affirmation day 7:
“Our connection to that power and to others is based on love and compassion”
Brené Brown

Affirmation day 8:

"Only the development of compassion and understanding for others can bring us the tranquility and happiness that we all seek".

Dalai Lama

Affirmation day 9: "When I am an observer, everyone is my teacher"

Anonimo

Affirmation day 10:
"Every act of love that I perform will raise the vibration of the universo"
Bhakti

115.

Affirmation day 11: "When the flight of others makes me happy I understood everything".

Anonimo

Affirmation day 12:
"Everything changes when I surrender, everything flows when I let go".

Anonimo

Affirmation day 13:
"Everything comes when it's time, everything heals when I accept"
Anonimo

Love

Affirmation day 14: "Do what I love, love what I do, be what I love, love what I am"

Anonimo

Affirmation day 15:
“Absolutely everything that happens to me is to awaken my conscience and follow my evolution”.
Dalai Lama

125.

Affirmation day 16:

"I look at the light in others and treat them as if it is the only thing I see in them".

Wayne Dyer

127.

Affirmation day 17:
“If we can't do great things, yes we can do small things with great love”.
Teresa de Calcuta

129.

Affirmation day 18: The revolution of love begins with a smile

Teresa de Calcuta

127.

Affirmation day 17:

"If we can't do great things, yes we can do small things with great love".

Teresa de Calcuta

125.

Affirmation day 16:
"I look at the light in others and treat them as if it is the only thing I see in them".
Wayne Dyer

129.

Affirmation day 18: The revolution of love begins with a smile

Teresa de Calcuta

131.

Affirmation day 19:
“I give each word roots in my heart”
Alejandro Jodorowsky

133.

Affirmation day 20: "Let's relate to others with a smile, because the smile is the beginning of love".

Teresa de Calcuta

135.

Affirmation day 21:
"The love that is received and transmitted, is that beautiful feeling that annihilates our egoism".
Alejandro Jodorowsky

Thank you for your purchase,
I hope the painting and making the affirmations has been useful for your life, leave me comments how your experience was so that it may inspire others. a fraternal hug.
Ariadna Saira.

www.ingramcontent.com/pod-product compliance
Lightning Source LLC
LaVergne TN
LVHW010609160826
845677LV00013B/3317

* 9 7 9 8 7 3 7 0 5 1 1 9 8 *